# BIOGRAPHY

OF MY

*Death Sentence*

LEGION

Order this book online at www.trafford.com
or email orders@trafford.com

Most Trafford titles are also available at major online book retailers.

Printed in the United States of America.

ISBN: 978-1-4669-7616-0 (sc)
ISBN: 978-1-4669-7618-4 (hc)
ISBN: 978-1-4669-7617-7 (e)

Library of Congress Control Number: 2013900429

*Trafford rev. 01/15/2013*

 www.trafford.com

North America & international
toll-free: 1 888 232 4444 (USA & Canada)
phone: 250 383 6864 ♦ fax: 812 355 4082

*Beware of Cults*

Preachers come without invitation
At your door find the bell they ring
Knock on front door sometime either's
They crawl like snake making their ways
You taste flattery your mind get delighted
Their words touch like experienced dancer
Elated soon with eagle you fly in the sky
By their nice words you dance in the rain
Their creativity to lies reaches its zenith
Make your heart warm to melt like candle

Feed your soul with balloons full of air
Their words are seeded deep in your heart
Cult member want to control your thought
To become your life your goal your mentor
The cult ideology is to become like a couth
Use religion to smear ideology dissenter.

*Dedication*

This book is dedicated to children's who were and still are victims of cults. Especially children's that had travel the same path of misery on a daily basis. Hope this book finds many broken heart broken family and bring comfort and hope to everyone. You are not alone traveling this horrific path. My hope from this book is to give you strength hope and faith to conquer your own battlefield of sorrows despairs and anxieties. My goal is that you find support knowing that you are not alone and someone understand your situation and struggles.

Here are too poems that I composed I thought it would be a good start for my book also encouragement, comfort, relief before you entering the devastating zone of the choice of my parents among other's

*A dying rose*

Life is the symbol of a precious, delicate unique circle
And a professional to his sculpture forging the present
Where the result is depending on good or bad cycle
To portray that existence could be joyful or lamented.

Just like a rose die separated from her source of life
All those who suffer from abuses and molestations
Secretly, their hearts bleed, and are where torment rife
Become a source of despair heavy load of frustrations.

Their scares in associate the past toward theirs future
To this question crossing theirs minds at time why me?
Do I deserve to live with this pain, atrocity, displeasure?
Is like a vast desert where nobody has heard the plea.

Alas, these dueling atrocities of pain every day resurface
Ruining the existence of peace, above all trustfulness
Harvesting confusion anger and a sense of being unsafe
Rejected, left behind because of lack of been trustiness.

*Love Bring Joy*

Every day we have a weakness and need for love
Every day we find irresistible to be in harmony
Every day we are attracted with beauty above
Every day we choose thing about how to agree.

Love is the path how we learn to find the irresistible
Love is the path to unity to expand peace and keen on
Love is the path to hold steady our dreams acquirable
Love is the path to appreciate things that come upon.

Never say no to tenderness be devoted rapid like a dove
Never say no to feeling for his voice develop friendship
Never say no to affection holding dearly treasure trove
Never say no to amity be partial enjoy to be partnership.

# Danger of Cult's Hypnotism

Every day we make good and bad choice
Not to be call by everyone wise brilliant smart
Some of them groomed planned and voice
Till days arrives were solution too late to come
As tears Form River of pain, chaos bring suffering
Surprise disgusted denouncing the evil outcome
Lack of knowledge of pure evil control is reveling
Bad education even hypnotism partially is to blame
Parental advice above all appear miscommunication
Sings of dysfunctional trouble personality ashamed

Individual living in denial double life face delusion
The perpetrator is always known as gentle incapable
When doing his horrors vested in multiple personality
Mind control create event, choice some time irreversible
Never the less conduct these perpetrators to insanity.
In full extend of craziness vividly dying for manipulation
For a cult mental disorder sociopath leaders
There are so many ways and evil tactics
Often in our world been daily use to exploit
Influence our world sectarian disease didactic

Promises of distinguish cult leader adroit
As their cool prudence sensitive selfishness
Along with quick thinking project perception
Fool nations about the unreachable and possible
Making real or ambiguous references inception
Event that is the beginning or first part of the stage
Play by an exceptional orchestra experienced pianist
Poker card at hand using time subsequent events
Some with honesty but infiltrates with dishonesty
Deceptive fraudulent and dispose to cheat to make assent

Defraud deceive also promise to undertake effort to give
Making prophetic statement prediction or tell in advance
Firsthand in his knowledge of state and emotions to live
To rule with a lofty proud gait often in an attempt to prance
Under pressure transform dictator ready to shrive.

Born into a cult here a part of the stories of my life
My family and other's

# *The beginning*

It was a perfect family until one day my parents decided that the society was turning to the wrong avenue. In the middle of the night fleeing like criminal avoiding all others members of families, pack up the rest of their belongings in the secrecy and the quiet of the time were only wilds animals are running the street and the raven in search for some to eat for their existence. One motive strive them to do so, how to avoid and save us from a dam world and find a safe haven in return to give us a kingdom were they will enjoy the grow of their children's. Looking to be safe without having to deal with their responsibility and give to their action justifications of doing so. By all, mean avoiding all guilt and remorse to have done it the way they choose to do so. Their marriage is not what is the best, among the problems is the one of too much time at the bar also gambling not enough time spend with the kids and money to raise the "kids". On the way toward some unknown territory, rules, style of life quietly they had surrender their soul and families to what we call hazard. During the day of travel and tiredness mixed with feeling and driven by anxiety, my parents endorse the ultimate sacrifice assured on false promises of a safe Heaven that turn out to be a trap in their life and our own also. To a turning, point where there will be a no return. Listening to false prophets and charlatans predicting chaos and miseries ready to form and fall upon this universe because of it crimes also to save the remaining of what they have called faith my parent blindly and with "faith" embrace all their lies . . . Upon our first day in the what we had to call from now on "our family" totally separated of our parent from each other brothers and sisters the boys live with the boys and the girls with the girls giving to stranger by our parent entrusted they given them the green light to raise and do whatever they decided to do with us. As time are fleeing away and the pain associate with the separation from us within our parents also from our own siblings, our parents really felt more and more comfortable in their style of life. It became a "normal" way of life for them but for us kids it became hell on earth what we call the end of our very own existence. From now on with no parent around and freely giving away there is very I should say no supervision at all. It is the free for all and like a tiger without pity toward is victim wounded and torn up don't saddle down until no remain is left to be see there we had to be and lived among criminals. I was 6 month old at the time and did not appreciate at all to be separate from my mom at that age. My others siblings were confuse and scare, also wondering, suffering from the separation that became final, cruel without any return. God is demanding perfection and of course, you could not join the cult or be with or in the presence of god if you possess some Earthly good. My parent had sold all of their belonging, gives to the cult the fruit of their long hours of work, and suffers in exchange of a promised holy land. Education was the main topic of the leader in the cult, and was one of the most ferried one. Not education the way the society understands and refers to but a twisted one where evil become well and good become so evil. By all mean to avoided and combat against every day with a precision were only the leader knows how to approach and define evil. With the expectation that all members even children's, infants, babies fulfill his orders with exactitude, timely executed. The fear of been reprimanded or apprehended by the leader is a very real treat and to make sure that these treat does not come into the path of the adult and of my parent they ensure that they accomplish all exigency and will of the leader no matter how stupid and dominant it may sound and look. Adults and parents had surrender all of their right also stolen all natural liberty given to each babies at birth from their children's taking hostage against their will and forcefully had impose stranger to take care of theirs responsibilities. In the mitt of all that moral suffering here was coming the worse at the hand of these strangers that did not have any consciences at all what so ever. For the most of the part the one put in charge of the kids did not have no education on how to take care and raise children's. Nobody on Earth know better in the personal view of a leader of a cult, but itself no law stand in front of an iron wall and surely no law enforcement also has the right to interfere or impose the law to verify if adequate care education and welfare of the children's are met. The leader considers he above all law. In his safe heaven publicly in the compound the leader were he take the full extends of his craziness into making himself first to be a short of a king also a master. Respect is one of is criteria, exigency become also a duty for everyone to knowledge and obey his usurped authority as the only safe way toward how direction and decisions should be thought in the new style of life of his faithful and to adhere in all form no matter what to the leader commend. Here is the start of a painful, horrible and so shameful way of raising "kids". A free for all situation where the bigger is always a winner and were a child is always put in harm way and constantly under attack from the leader and all of the supporters of the leader who themselves are a bunch of criminals abusers. The wolf has the form of the cheap and the cheap less parents among others adults are misguide and solely sold their children giving up on their only responsibility submit to the will and desire of a dictator. Many time the tactic of fear is use for a way to bring everyone to submission and to ensure that no one in the group interfere and pose any kind of "trouble" show off any discomfort or disagreement. For every order is a yes that is the expected response there is no place for logic nor compassion because this word is to be seen no were in their dictionary nor discipline. There is no place for a "no" it's a "yes" in all what has been asked or expected from all the member who form the cult especially for innocent children's infants and babies whom are consider as the continuation of the cult. Taken at birth for an automatic adept who will live and die in the most miserable situation were only inhuman criminals activity take place there is no chance at all for these babies and children's and adolescents to grow at the space of the circle of their life. In another word infant has to act and behave like an adult otherwise he would be brought to the leader and all of his accomplices under submission no matter the way or means it's take to archive the evilness twisted mind of.

# Early childhood

My parents brought to this safe heaven under the pretext of morals and because they also choose to adhere to all of it, exigencies and demands surrendering all of us to these monsters in a cult were human rules and compassion does not exist. We were frail innocent and candid's "kids" also defend less here we had to be, not able to show or say anything of from the treatment giving to us and if we like it or dislike it onto our new style of life and to what happening to us. Our parent turns their back on us and to their ultimate duties on earth. Driving by the love of power and glory, the leaders proud of his success felt powerful upon innocent little infants, baby, boy and girls. Having all control and decisions quickly these monsters savored every minutes and hour that went by. The most critique thing is that they were free to do as please without having to give any feed back to the parents.

In the beginning, since they were so "poor" then later all of our childhood we were deprive from early child vaccinations and doctor routine. This served also as a cover up to the early child abuses and molestations, to cover up all form of abuses that took place while they were mandated to us by our parents. At this point, that was a great victory for the leader. He now was fully in charge and in control of the situation. Demanding from us ultimate respect he wanted us to adopt him has our own and unique father, he expected that we accept it him as a loving and caring father, if we did not do well he did not care because he had stolen this role from our own parents and imposed it on us. One way or the other thing had to go his way and only his. At first glance and vision in my view and I am sure from the rest of my family it was the end. Devastation was no words and feelings could possibly describe the ocean of pains and despairs marking our every day of life. We were expose and under lamentable situation innocent submit totally blindly to the order and desire and in the hand of the wolf just like a sheep devoured by the wolf enjoying his victory toward an innocent and defend less poor babies infants boys and girls covered from is abuses victimize by it cruelties. We did not had the luxury of having diaper and the composition of what we use to call diaper was of cloth cut from a piece of sheet of what ever came first at hand. In addition, at an early age we had to wash our own diaper and I remember my little piece of wood were I use to scrub the remaining of my accident. That was the duties of every kid old enough to do so.

The compound itself was in the great North of Esterel, believe me when winter was there boy o boy it was a better cold and more door to abuses also tortures. It was like an opportunities and satisfaction from our abusers in a word as to put a fine touch to their evil doing. They were this room were we use to hang our coat and hat after each time coming back from saying the rosary coming from slay riding they would have a pleasure to lock us in the dark room bringing us into a total darkness dead feeling terrifying us and bring upon us some cruel and disproportioned punishments I am talking here about infants under 6 years of ages. To have more to their pleasure they would make some noise of chain play some macabre music and knocking on the wall. We had to stay in the room quiet without crying, up to when they opened the door and let us out. Sometime the noise was so scary that we wanted to pee in our pant but the scare of having to go through more physical and emotional abuse stop us from the disaster. Some time we just could help to avoid the disaster, for punishment we were again on our piece of wood and clean our "diapers". Remember here I am talking about infant of two-3-4-years of ages. While this was happening my dad was no were to be found and he was name to go begging for the food. At first no one wanted to give him food so he decided to dig into the disposal garbage of the big companies of food in Montreal to retrieve the very little of good that were throw away. He spends a lot of hour digging in the warm or cold weather. From what he found good and afterward was shorted by the older kids and later on by us also this was to be our food . . . Many time we had the same thing every day. I do remember that in the mist of all that we had receive some load and load of bananas so our recipe was very simple, Bananas for the morning bananas for diner and again bananas for super. They use to tell us that

God has giving us bananas and that His will was that this was what we were supposed to have for our diet. Everything was based on donation and believe me at first it was not very pleasant at all because most of the time the outside bad world did not know the growth of this very cult starting right into the society. We had to show that we were recognizant for the give that they had to present to us. When we got older, we still had to do the shorting of our own vegetable fruit and desert. Most of the day was spend in silence or if we were too small to realize what silence mean we were put into recollection until we had learn to not cry nor make noise. It was an expectation from our "monitors" who had very little patience that babies, infants boys and girls was to be educated as if they were already had reached the adult age. They were no question of acting like our own age. They had a lot of little house and they called these place "mission" and I do remember in one of them at the age of 3 years of ages I was deprive of eating all day because I did not know my hail Mary by heart. The moral torture and physical abuses had reach degrees were no one could even imagine including our own parents. The worse of all is that we were taking away from our parent for the rest of our life. It was like no end in the sight.

All alone walking barely understanding very little we had to be of a nature of an adult, it's was so impossible that every day it was a challenge were the bigger as always got their way and us the poor looser. Everything was based on believe that this was the holy will of God . . . . To the very start, the problem with the authorities and Government started and rushed into hidden place. At the time, I was only six month old so I am asking myself today how in the world I was keep without crying or making some kind of noise to show my need. May be it a good thing that answers does not flow like a river because it may be too hard and harsh to remember this time. All what I know is that we were placed and hidden under ground and also some time into some underground tunnel serving to pass the heating system for the main compound. We spend some long hour in theses hidden places and situation without even know and realize the real reason for what was happening at the time except for what they made us truly believe plenty good raison to justify themselves and their caring for us. Crying persecution by all mean wanted us to believe what they were doing, was for our own good and protection again evil people. The buggy man would grab us into a bad world take our body and soul to hell. Which really was not, but what we did not understand at the time is that their whole effort and the impositions of these abuses was only for their own business and deal. We had become things and were not considered and treated as human. I am sure that some of the older one remembers a lot more then I of what had taken place in those hidden place without no running water, electricity, and pitch black, molded and cool.

The effect of those traumas had only made us more vulnerable and makes us felt that we were completely at their mercy and their guises. With no mommy and daddy around to supervise the whole situation we were with the only feeling of been totally rejected from our own parents. This sentiment of rejection did not take a long time to take effect on us and give more pleasure and joy to our torturers. The more vulnerable we were to be the more it was a victory for these peoples without no conscience at all, and no dignity. For some reason my parent went through these difficult times and abuses themselves without seeing any wrong doing following blindly and in obedience to all the directive and will of the supreme leader. For now on for all the adult followers it became a way and style of living, relaxing and in peace with themselves having no bill to paid no real responsibilities and care. Just shut up and obey don't ask question always a yes to all the exigencies of the leader no matter if that what was asking from them make sense or not, as they were to live under the woes the king down of a brutal dictator secretly organizing his palace in accordance to all of his wish and vision. Interpreting situation life in general the leader had all power with their help, money and perseverance behind close door and secretly. The guru and ardent zealot did not have no respect what so ever toward any kind of Authorities from the outside world. We were brought up as thinking that police were demons came directly from hell and working together to destroy the work of God here on Earth, and that give them respect was wrong and a sin a way for sure toward damnation for eternity. Of course, no Authority would of challenge them because most likely it involved religion. No serious investigation as took form only some raids that only did help the cult to survive and cry out injustice persecution and miss understanding of their reason of existence. From far and only far away they would let these same Authorities come in after having hidden all evidence threatening to kill us if we talk and tell the truth. Of course very well organize and compose they had a perfect element in their hand by cutting us totally from the rest of the world. In other word, we were isolate from the real society into a non-society full of chaos, abuses and neglects. No camera, video television radio were allows and giving to us. We had to be detaching from the good of the Earth also from any form of affection of our parents brothers and sisters from dog and cat what we call in modern society pet. In order to do so they ensure that none of us could have the possibility of getting any of these earthly good vanity sensations and love all was to be reserve for God, nor ride the bus to school with other kids making friends connection with other kid of the opposite sex having the same age of us. Of course, to blame was the same bad world where it was not possible to receive a good Christian education. Education was a non-need because in the compound we were to be born live as a slave for the rest of our life.

As time when by a lot of abuse was taking form, to give themselves justification of the wrong doing on their part they were saying out laugh "these are only kids they won't remember nothing." Much time I recall having ear this statement from my abusers and every time I was saying to myself, I will prove you wrong. No matter how hard you tried to be good you just could never reach to their perfection guideline gold that has been expected from us kids. For some of us we were always in trouble, and most of the time it was the children's were the cult authorities knew that the parent were sold to the cause and became monk and nun. For other it was different especially if the parent of those kids were living on the outside world. They were still abuse but a lot less severely then the one whom parent was forming body and soul with the cult. Beating, molestation, mental abuse, verbal abuse, was our loaf of bread became a regular basis. With no supervision at all from adult non forming the cult well this had opened all doors and windows as for express in reading myself to cruelties barbarizes by only the most wanted criminal in the world untouchable because of been wise like a fox. Closely supervise and monitor every move of us kid's now adults were trained by criminal how to makes real lies sound good believable to be truth to Authorities and Law enforcement. The abuses that I am talking about are dating even before my family got involve without our consent in the cult. When my parent join the group I was the baby my brothers and sisters very little kids, we had to follow our parent choice share and live what they were allowing too happened to us like the food serve by them to us on our plate for our every meal. Let me tell you if you did not experiment despair well you should consider yourself lucky, because it a place where you can take my word on it you just don't want to be the victims nor the target or objects. To have to deal with the pain, anguish attributed to that plague and calamities into this very low place in life very quickly drive your soul in such of miserable place that all what you want to do is to die. After all we came to realize that we were born to die in this miserable empty place run by monsters and peoples of low class that all what they want and desire is to hurt kids broke and dismantle every family that as the bad luck to believe their lies to became victims of their evil thought. The leader desire intensified by barberries that only monsters can archive professionally I believe animal are incapable to do and reach at this level. In other word worse them all the most wilds animals that lives on our planet and would of scare us a great deal, if we met them face to face without any preparation. This comparison is just a little corner of the pain, fear, deception, anguish and hurt those girls and infants boys had to deal alone with no mommy and with no daddy. We swallow these assaults done onto our person becoming constantly a non-wanted human being sacrifice and morally kill resembling to a lamb in the hand of the butcher.

## Mysticisms

All the foundation of cult repose solely on the only basis that God appear to a man the leader and then transmit His will upon us through his mouth just like Moses way back in the old testament in the bible. Using every element very well calculated supported by other charlatans nothing works better then blinds sheep's from whom the sheep less are guide by their nose to pasture and prosperity that only the leader has the power and the knowledge to do so. For the leader it's a way of seeing like he got the ultimate power he is a King a somebody because in the net of all of his plans and calculations he will be able to live like a king without to have to work for all of his life. In the other hand the adept are like his personal slave where he is the lord of the ring the sovereign the all almighty a divinity. Respect, he does not know this word with an odious extravagance he wants respect and imposes himself upon is faithful with a rule of iron. Having no pity no mercy and no common sense toward the understanding of the basic of human right except when it touch to his authority control and power. Money power and sex this is the ultimate dreams and nothing stand of on his pat when he studies all of the angle of the situation studying on how to take advantage to the maximum of the situation.

Using religion as made more them one happy and rich. It has come down to, listen to me follow blindly and never ask question. Never doubt or put into taught anything he will ask you to do and make sure it's executed in the 5 bar on the minute otherwise you are reprimanded suspended up to put into quarantine like a bad apple undesirable. The mentality of the leader was no matter whom as the authority may be he is a saint and even a pervert the authority is sacred until we did not understand this in the cult we will turn in a circle. Right there you see the form of demand of the leader toward is devoted members to adhere with blind obedience to all of is order or wishes and desire. Also he denounce himself as who really he is but it's too late for the fervent member to even began to realize the situation already brain washed and welling to do whatever the order or commends are. They have swallow already too much of cool aid in a sense mentaly speaking and for them if he tell them that the color blue is red then it automatically turn the color he told them no question ask even if it sound completely out of line and contest. Freely ripe of their common sense absorbing the reject of their personalities, responsibilities, fervent and willingly they have found what they are looking for an easy way out. Becoming like robots without no vertebral only working on commends to make them act like rag, to the point that they do not see anything wrong doing in on an everyday basis for the rest of their life. As soon that, there is a very small doubt or a very little disturbance the leader was all in agitation and for him to gain the momentum is something very critical. Any means and tools is good to be used especially the ones that look goods and innocents are the one to be the most successful and were the most of the poison of the leader in giving to his faithful cheap less and having already surrender their whole being and soul to its commends. At this point, they do not give a care about the impact done onto the life of others the society as a living member but willingly separated and considering them above any one on Earth. No law authority other them their own and the one put in place by the leader are existing and standing in front of charlatan that use mysticism to betray and rob all and everything that fall into their hands.

The name of God become a tool and a door to many situation complots were the leader write is new bible and commandments expectations also the deviance in between is preaching and is actions. For example in order to surrender all of his adepts under is guise well the first thing he does is preaching the detachment of the good of the Earth. What that means and does is that the leader demand the perfection of is faithful and purity in the living of the bible base on the word and will of God to abstract and enable his follower to come back and go somewhere else in the world of damnation and corruptions. Once the adept have freely given all of his possession legitimate right to own possess dispose of his life in making decisions on how to be irresponsible careless on what bases do this adept have to make a return back to society? Nothing what so ever this is the danger of the existence of all cults because it brings some disaster where the consequences have no limits. If the adept have children well of course, he would care enough to step down and face the reality but more likely, he will surrender them to the leader on false pretext of the will of God. The bible is for now on use to destroy life also family and society and to disrupt at the maximum the circle of life. The most crucial thing that takes form here is that God never has anything bad to say about the leader. He is incapable of making any neither errors nor imperfections, if something is going wrong or is just about to happen then right away the adepts are the one to be blames. The leader use pretext like message from God, fear, guilt to impose all of his guilt his responsibility on the shoulder his sheep less members. Blindly with the conviction of the truth that given to the members of the cult, the person swallows everything and takes for cash without investigation all the false mysticisms and ruse from the leader like the solo and inevitable will of God. My experience on this subject is that the more the order or the demand is out of touch and realities the more the faithful of the sect follow the directive and the commend from its leader. The more they surrender their will to the wish and desire of the leader the more they are on the road toward perfection. God always demand perfection and faith to all of his fervent sheep less devoted children's as for gage of loyalties and allegiance to its rules and obligations. The ultimate sacrifice is requiring no question no doubt tolerated. Blind obedience is the key number one that makes all adepts of the cult to surrender their common sense, personalities, moral, ethnic and to make them loose realities and touch to the real world of whom they make part.

They are willingly at the mercy and guise of their only master and the only one thing they want to know and live for. At first, while the cult was still at the blouson and fresh out of the net the leader had the tendencies to have more message and vision from God. As time went by and the sheep less followers are getting tired of having the same message and dictation from the leader and his rule demand and sacrifices the urgencies of finding another outcome is becoming more important and the preoccupation in the mind of the leader is to keep control of the situation. No matter what is the cost and sacrifices from his followers the urgency and preoccupation of the leader is to maintain his role of power money and control. Smart enough to seed from nothing a vast kingdom he has to constantly be aware and on the guard among his own follower. Sometime violence is a tool utilized to show power control exigencies and submission. Other time kindness is use but this is rarely and only when allow and permit controlled very well calculated for the need or satisfaction of seeing himself in charge and in control. For the most part, he has recourse to its own mean and extravagance to obtain and to surrender everything that stood on his way. If problem occur with the judicial system no problem he has the answer for everything. Using the bible grabbing everything that could be useful to confuse the judicial system who weakness demonstrates little knowledge on religion. Citing whatever phrase or quote perfectly organize like a game of poker at the guise of the leader hand into what he base himself and justify his conduct and believe. For the most of the time Jesus only interest is to have direct line of conversation dictation with the supreme leader, He do not put aside the idea source from the outside which are calculated well groomed supervised choose only the one that could of be of interest and a tool toward his success. Cleaver in the realization of his master plan and this is to become an empire and strong kingdom in itself where he is the king master and supreme leader.

While in a other hand he do not want to have to listen to anyone nor acknowledge other authorities, full of himself from time to time the leader realize that he do need help, not the kind of help he really need but a fake and odious pretension of taking himself above anyone and any laws. His preference will go toward people that are nice globule simple of mind have very little instruction with false religion mental deviation. The dream for the leader is to found someone that no one want to associate themselves with but naïve and credulous, easy to seduce ready to accomplish and to crush down anything that stand on their way to become accomplice under the supreme leader guide and rule a so called powerful majesty. Above all simple, frustrate people whom are dying to be a star.

The need of exploitation and control become out of control and touch with the present on everything and everyone that compose his Universe more specifically above all the one making the circle of his pretended holiness, like a while animal looking to satisfy his instinct the thirst of the leader turn him like a dictator. For the leader he as give himself a so call authority putting himself above all laws and basis right that come with each one of us at our birth. It is nothing for him to come right out without any guilt or bad feeling and start to insult or accuse his own personnel's breaking and destroying family children's in a physical and especially in a mental way. On this subject, there will be a lot to say because this is one of the key toward success in all cults or groups were the members are keep isolated keep into a deep trance of ignorance. Surrender by force also defends less especially among the children's who have the bad luck to be born into one of these organizations. For the adult adept well it become the will of God on Earth, but for the children's well this is a beginning of the end where ether the wrap or the goodness of the same god trough the choice and decisions and the parents come from and trough. His adults followers see nothing wrong into what they are witnessing and living on an everyday basis and style of live. It has become normal and the way of guiding their life through the horrible outside world and like a butterfly before becoming a giant insect had to go and live in a cocoon. It is the same scenario and process for a cult but unlike the butter fly free a cult is operated by a dictator where liberty freedom surrender without no coming back at the hand a monster. Deliberately making choice of adherence to the full extends of the rule exigency and will of the leader. Diffuse is venin with abundance onto honest adults at one time in their life becoming monster themselves human garbage. They chose to be guide blindly following orders given by a dishonest human who interest is toward himself and how to get power glory sex and control that also is looking for an easy way out without having to work but by putting all of his followers at work for him and his kingdom. Reflecting all of his responsibilities and need in his life onto the one of his followers who without question adhere and seriously take for cash all of the exigencies of the leader and make a duties to fulfill his will. The leader becomes the will of god for them to take away their only responsibilities raising their own blood and flesh, their kids. Where there is a will there is also a way, this say goes onto to sense, for the parents who accept to adhere to the rules and regulations of a dictator where common sense does not exist and far from been respected they could not even come close to understand nor wanted to live this kind of life. The parent freely are imposing upon innocents and defend less children's, infants also baby a miserable life. Desperately without the support and love from their parents, no word of encouragement no love kiss and understanding the connection with what they are be force to live create an ocean of despair. Rapidly take the same child into a transformation where some time the thought of suicidal seem to be the remedies because of the traumas and abuses impose onto these same individual.

I do recall that most of my abusers where very liberal toward themselves and very strict and exigent toward their so-called possession. Many time after we have been molested and hit by our perpetrator I have use to heard "these are only kid they will not remember" and every time that I've heard this sentence in my heart I would reply, "I would prove you wrong". A determination I believe is what keep me going in life because in my childhood between many other's they were nothing to live for and everything were taken away from us including our right of existence. That include to be raise like normal kid in family and with love all that because of greediness, selfness, impose on me and many others in the world and the prime cause of this most of the time is to be blame upon religion and to what an individual adult put all of is believing into also his faith. The problem that I have encounter through my decision of leaving the cult was that I was all alone to travel this path of anger also rage. I've never have any words of encouragement from my parent or my usurper that wanted me to respect them as my legitimate parent as a child trough all these year of abuse they suddenly forgot who I was and from the day of my rupture from the movement I became a traitor. In the eyes of theses monsters a non-existent but the worst, I had to pick up the pieces try to put them together. Consume with the feeling that I was born but rejected by my natural parents in the name of RELIGION. I have to say here that not all religion are bad and identical, no not at all this is far from realities and of my believe. However, one has to recognize the danger and severe traumas that religion can impose on individuals and society. Infant that are growing into an atmosphere of exploitation from adult whom utilize religion to perpetrate their evilness abuses in all form, sexual, mental, spiritual, physical, above all has their legitimate right stolen from them at a very young age endure traumas that society as a whole has to endure because the long term affect them. We are all depending to each other's, if one of the members is dysfunctional because of this kind of tribulation well the society as a corps has to endure its consequences destructive for the entire life of the victims. As I said this, it is very important here to say that in life we all have choice and decisions to make. Not everybody responds the same way and with the same tactic this is why we are calling a universe. For my part I firmly believe that we has victims has only too choice to make, the one to be a survivors pick up ourselves bravely continues to face all challenges laying in front of us or play the victims where this outcome only serve to make life more miserable and ended up to force living into the gather. Why I am saying this now is for everyone to realize the magnitude of the problem also of his or her long terms consequences. I do realize also that not everyone has the same capacities. Also among my experience and from what I witnessed is that the younger the victim is surrender in a situation where no contact at all is made with the civilize world whom the cult keep a led on the children's infants as a token the future of his cult the more difficulties and hard work is real and present. The age of the individual is very crucial, unique also because it engrave a mark into as for say a false personality and will onto the victim to the point that in the living of his routine into what we call normal society. The challenge and intensity of the requirement most of the time is overwhelming in many case driven to despair following by the sense of a non-wanted. Religion has its good side as for it bad sides I agree with this but much time when religion is the cause of real evilness from my own experience it is ignore untouched by fear and totally covers up by authority and churched. It is only after many years some time a lifetime that the story of abuses come to the surface and hit the news and the society. Even if the society are aware of the problem earring the story of the victims that reached the level of survivors at an adult age the making of the case is very hard to be put into evidence in court of law because of the laps of time. Some time it laid aside and simply goes without trial because not enough proof and evidence. The leader knows very well the consequence of permitting allowance of camera camcorder television. In some case, isolation total with the public school system goes toward his advantage, taste, perverted desire. In the case of my family and many other's this became the sad reality, deprive from everything that could have been of a help in our life the leader viciously perpetrate all of his crime on us with the peace of mind and conscience that no one ever could come after him or the cult. In order for the leader to succeed trough what he is calling a "career" he had to fine tone all of his approach and talent into a mental game were religion mysticism and sheep less followers melt together. The vast majority of the public get mislead by using their ignorance also good faith to push to the maximum for his own benefits without scrutiny been suspected of doing so nor been investigated, given him all the tool power and advantage over the society. This is where non-profit organization come and take form into a cult were the destruction and demolition of many personality family take form alive also were chaos and frictions will survive among members in the cult and members that walk away from the cult also long after the dead of the older personal of the cult. In order to belong to a cult normally you have to detach yourself of the good of the Earth your family uncle aunt the list goes on, give the revenue of the sale to the compound give up your love for family and children's values then and only then you can archive the gold of becoming perfect. The use of mysticism get it's root from the use of the bible, the more the leader know the bible the more of the guaranty of success is laying in the vision and pat of the leader. With bible verse all leader play with emotions of its faithful and sadly these sheep less are depending on how the leader feel well and that could be for them good news or bad news. It's the same thing as to be born without feeling freedom and just been like a living thing to choose to listen to charlatans and to confine all your believe and faith into their fantasies. The cult leaders is smart enough to control and find way to dupe and enslave other's to become rich at their expand. The bible in some case do not belong into everyone's hand, especially a control freak person full of himself and in some case the leader paranoiac that believe and make is adept believe an uprising world is soon will form to crush them. As soon some trouble come across his pat the leader do not appreciate he is persecuted the end of the world would soon ring upon their head or the whole Universe. To avoid such of tragedies well the leader ask of his faithful more perfection zeal faithfulness and conviction to confront and to bring down all danger that may struck the cult his leader also them and by doing so they are accomplishing the holy will of god. In some case, which was my case and many, more of us once upon a time in the cult the leader would make us studies the foundation of the cult and give us some quiz onto chapter every Sunday night. This was to prepare us to give the right answer if summoned by the people of the outside world with question of interest to ensure all response is identical and uniform. This comfort zone avoid him some embarrassment with circle of friend also with the media the common sense in the real world. Really it is not enough to have destroy family and morals but the leader chose to go further in his evilness impose himself not only upon is cheap less faithful but onto the real world all in the name of RELIGION and FAITH. However, a fool "the leader" feels is how the whole universe has to felt and act accordingly to the leader fantasies and witches. Taking everyone and everything for only what the leader can take out for him and the cult. Religion become a tool toward the destruction of his sheep less followers and a knives well sharpened and very well cover up with lies a life style of treachery. You only notice that you got trap also wounded and take advantage of only after the fact and the bleeding of yourself because the leader will demand from his sheep less that they give everything. Family, land, car, heritage, the list goes on under the guise of false mysticism interpreted by the leader the only way toward perfection the only way to be pleasant to God almighty. The seed of the deception take much form and face unique becoming a shame also a blame game between the ex-member and the cult. Deplorably it's only after the falling into the deception masteries piece of evilness set up that some members come to awake in the cult working hard to break free toward the civilize society but the damage some time are irreversible and last for a life time. The mea culpa, resentment, rage, deception are the fruit that false religion, mysticisms and cult bring into our society included everyone's of us in deferent degree but to most of its deception is felt by the victim of such of a criminal act and design associate with the pain of having been miss lead. The big problem here is when false religion and cult destroy family. If an adult by free choice choose to join a cult because of it believe well this must be respect a guess but when you have innocents baby, infants, adolescent well this become a total new story. This is not free choice and will of these people but a enslaver situation where all the human right are taken away and were the seed of deception is glomming and fertile.

*Child exploitation*

As time goes on and shapes the mole, nothing stands on the way. We are turning like "livings things" where no feeling need of respect is ever due. Our routine already shape and dictated directed by organize criminal become our daily mensal bread. Disguised artistic calculated are mastering commends by the puppeteer every element and will of the leader is to be executed right away without any question. Child labor becomes a random I must say a free for all. After all, we do not exist as human so give good conscience and justification for all exploitation. Green light in every desire of the leader forces into submission to his orders accomplished. Using kindness in rare occasion rudeness, almost every chance and sadistic means is the breath of the perpetrator. No doctor visit allowed in circumstance where abuse or negligence has created some irresponsible reprehensible actions on the behalf the adult. We are born to live in the cult and to die in the cult. The notion of us "kids" becoming one day adult does not fit very well in the timing and denial of the leader and associates. To make us work have one advantage and it is to become rich at the expense of innocents little children's. Child exploitation was on all form use to maintain control and power. Mental abuses where on all expansion humiliation calling of name was a daily meal serve with no regard for our feelings. The worst thing for the mind of a child is being call stupid. Since we were not considering as human being, it was not matters were or when the slaying took place was perpetrated. Adults project their evilness lacks of patience on any justification in the "object" that stood in front of them. Education was preliminary in many cases considered loss of time. Making the "child" believe that he or she is inclining more too manual work then intellectual, they will never amount to nothing intellectually except to be active at a very young age working like a slave. Submit to long hours of prayers little time for relaxation force to work a living imposes on us. In the early stage of the cult, the leader and associate had many involvements with the "justice department". Every time that strange event were too happened taking place we were always hidden in wood nearby or in underground place. These underground had no electricity no running water pitch black they were no bench we were oblige to sit on the ground. To cover up the place where we were hidden a little statue of Mary was set up as camouflage to distract all agile regard from the hidden horror. Yet no parents were around to supervise the treatment render to their kids. They had given their kid to God and now all what they have to do is to trust blindly and execute their daily task without asking question or reason. In this infernal dark place our imagination was running wild how the world is, evil the injustice commit again not us but the leader was outrageous. We considered ourselves like been own by living for die for the leader our will was slowly taking and put in reverse working against our real identities. The sentiment of abandonment the reality of been rejected was at that time well-grounded and I am sure we all had the same despair and anguish. The leader its associate stranger to our family became the rule with no conscience the lamb was at the mercy of the wolf. At the summer camp in the wood among the bears and wild animal existed here we where every day expose to negligent situation. At the heart of the problem, we did realize the depth of internal dead. Breading the air was for most of the time another occasion given to the perpetrator to commit is crime. During summer time at the camp, we were living a primitive life. Electricity was not present and for showers the nice cold river. If we had the bad chance to wet our sleeping bag well the next thing is we had to be throw in to the river zipped into the sleeping bag. We had to make our way out between rocks to the shore; this was a way to wash the sleeping bag all at once. These treatment was giving to us at a very young age as we got older well the new need in tactic was urgent need. It was never the same every day we could expect any disaster or a better situation in time. Depending upon the disposition and feeling of adult supervisor here was the schedule for our day. Work was the prime cause for our existence so no question to play. Silence was necessary except for occasional time where allowed to speak and sing. Wiesel was not appropriate purely evil, when apprehended to do so we were asking to stop. An innocent pleasure became a door to be the devil seeing him into dance onto our lips. Sometime the punishment was to get our face wash up with gravel to make sure we learn our lesson. At all, time when walking from destination to other destination we were in file divided by too. We had to be serious not make anything out of the normal otherwise, were told so and reprehended. We were to live life like grow up adult never giving a chance to our age to show excitement happiness. In rare occasion if we had been judge good in behavior we were allowed more time of what called recreation. We grow up into a short of concentration camp were the Nazi in world war too was dictating making all rule.

This was a contrast between lie became reality from what our parent choose to bring us there at first place nothing but lies had to convince our parent. In the mint of evilness the associate of the cult leader had invented a system where we had to care a card into our pocket. Every time we have been found guilty of wrongdoing, they punched the card and we had to make sure we do not lose it. At the end of the week, we had to present our card representing our evilness and receive our sentence. If too many point counted well the fair equitable punishment was strait to bed. If exceeding the expectation it was half of the evening in church and other half in bed. Prejudice was rampant and obvious, they dint like you or was in a crappy mood you were more done. They were too pole in the compound on how to deal with children's. The first one is the parent of the children's that associate themselves willingly to the group the others children's where the parent where still in the outside bad world. Not every kid had the same treatment although very similar in the separation and education but less physically abuse. At one time, we were at least over 80 boys and 70 girls living under their control. The rule was who care for the children totally sold to the cause and watchful for the one that parents had feet in and out. Even in this situation either way none of us had the right to have any short of instrument that could eventually been uses as evidence of abuse. Money Power sex and control is the heart of cult forming greed is necessary and pretension is the key. Abuse of power is nothing new and history will repeat itself the more an individual with a sick mentality his given power the greatest are the result. The longer we let go abuses and wait the more difficult situation become the more door kept opened the more idiot are free to walk in and out. Control environment at the hand of a dictator in noting more a disaster soon or later we have to deal with the result. Their influence grows to a disproportionate out of control mad man ideology that has to conquer the whole world. Cult presents them as savior only way out run by fear deception but presented as unique solution. Childs abuses have been source of multiple problem resulting image like taking a strait rule and bended to a deform form where nothing make sense any more. I am specifically talking about close groups that isolate themselves from the rest of the world. In every family and circumstance, we could find child abuse but specifically talking when isolate groups of adult are forming there this is other story. This is what we all had to live I am talking about children's of cult. Is the right of children's of cult is given representing themselves to choose to be respect? No were becoming victims of dupe's lays exploitations. Most of cult regard children's as their continuation especially for the leader it becoming a duties to make sure that his herd are well grounded. I am not saying that all religion and groups are bad I am specifically talking about close group where it is difficult for any authority to investigate. This clarification is important because we cannot put everyone in the same basket. Been abuse in the name of God is nothing less than a coward that does not know what to do with his life but smart enough to rule and conduct is way around without having to work. In most of language of cult "the work" is utilize often no matter how far the distance between each one of them they use the typical language. The work of God was predominant in the language of our late guru. I remember when I was a child I never could enough to be pleasant to god. It was the same situation for all children's in the cult. Besides working there come the time were we had to spend hours arm across in the chapel on our knee. I remember one year when the leader of the sect brought to justice because of refusing to obey a court order. This court order was to return kid to their dad that had split from the movement and had obtained legal custody of his children. We spend that night praying for this criminal so God would protect him. The next morning for tank, you he sends a message to us stating that we did not prayer hard enough. Saying that God love the prayers of children's but because of our lack of fervor, God did not answer our prayer. This statement was the nail in the coffin for us here we had spent the night up praying and still we could achieve any good. Exploitation does not only exit in the sexual physical field but also in the spiritual way. The list of physical abuse could go on my goal here is not as much to talk about the abuse rather to try to find solution. By sharing some of my story may be I will be able to help a family event one individual in need. The important is to get the story out for everyone to read learn and hopefully do not fall into the same trap. Cults are very active and always try to recruit others victims this is why beware of false prophet.

# *Mind control*

Living less than one roof with no freedom follower of the cult are unable to survive by their own. Rule is giving obeys with instance regardless of the majority of existing laws. The only prophet to heart is from now on the leader and immediate associate. Rank does not matter if the leader mock or praise you is all a due you just stood there and receive order. When it is time for a child to be raise in this kind of environment everything, step of his life deform and torn nothing left for him. For adult this becomes an easy way out freely adopted wanted. Mind control is easily on when the target is at very young age. This is the reason why the leader separated the child from their parents. By doing so, he ensures that no matter kind of situation arise; he would always have the upper hand on the situation. Nothing is more trustworthy in is mind then the word of an adult versa a child. Most of adult would believe the adult first then the child but after close examination, they finally come to believe the child. By then the damage done and the result in some circumstance are irreparable. Cults generally are cleaver and wise because their interest drove them to act and impose only toward one individual and goal. This give little place for the child who has misfortune to fall into this situation because been under age. Repetition and imposition of the same act routine work prayer have nothing but one thing for goal. This is to make sure that the individual come to a point that he is not capable to think for himself any more by consequence become like dependent subordinate. The will of God become automatically the will of the leader no matter its circumstance or stupidity it is necessary due. For children's born raise into this environment, the damage is greater and the effect last for the rest of his or her life. Depending on the personality of the child, have degree and vulnerability. The more the child surrender without force the more he or she is given favor the same for the child who is rebellious the more they do not accept the treatment the more they are in trouble. Personality destroy life torn nothing stand in front of this injustice toward innocent being. The leader realizes that to control a group the first thing he has to do is to ensure that there is no way out. He makes sure that the adept realized that this is their life and if ever they separated themselves from the movement is their dead and damnation. Isolation persuasion dictation is without limit with no regard supported by denial on the behalf of the leader. The thing that count is to ensure nuisance and Laws are ignore put aside in the mind of the adult parent who are active members.

When this is archive, the show is ongoing and the result amazing and flourishing for the leader. Children's become the possession of the leader and for the parent to see their own children's become for them a privilege. This controls any leaks that may occur between the child and his parent. Time of reunion usually is limited and under scrutiny if suspicion is in doubt this is termination automatically of the privilege. As a tree corrected at young age to grow strait, the same rule has to be in place for the development of a child. In a place like a cult, what crocket become strait the same goes for the opposite. Dependency bring slavery and exploitation this in mind the leader vigilantly work as his king down is built upon solid foundation. There is no place for self-discover talent everything turn around the leader what the leader say and think. Sermon exhortation retreat is tool in the disposition of the leader to control the expansion of his structural materialized dream. Children has become adult automatically are not allow to live their childhood live in family nor discover their identity. By doing so the damage of the brainwash is more complete difficult to break because this is all what children's of cult know. One day the sky is splendid and because the leader is down it become a raining day although

it is sunny out there. Then mind control has made all is assent and
the power of the leader increase in value and demand. Everything
works on order to execute by any mean and way. With this in
mind the children's of cult never know what to expect because the
abnormal become for them normal. No education on wrongdoing
because notion of good and bad been change. Trained to think
like a "thing" gladder then a person the brain of children's of cult
are programmed to obey on commend. With no parent around to
supervise activity, the leader has upper hand on sexual orientation
desire and execution of his "possession". Sadly, much more deviance

is the outcome of this short of abuse become open door to deplorable act. The leader knows it is easier to blame a kid then to take his own responsibility. This means that the guilt and shame totally the responsibility of the leader projected upon his victims. Yet never satisfy to torment his victim he makes sure that by fear and in some rare occasion by kindness the child is been force to stay his loyal "thing". Every time some suspicion occurs and suspected rapidity for cover up is a must and new torment for the "thing". Remember this is the height of evilness by isolating his "target" from his parent and the outside world the leader ensure his way into the own life of an innocent kid. Education well the less the "target" has some the better is for the safety of the cleaver criminal leader. To make good face and appearance to avoid confrontation with the Laws he make sure the basic respected. Most of the instructors are his own "thing" at one time that became adult deprive also from education do not possess a solid ground in education to become teachers. The leader make sure to befriend some low class frustrated educators and in some case persuade them to join the movement. Some of the educator is parenting himself or herself that joined the group who children's are in the compound. Either way the leader is on top of the situation making plant to ensure that, his laws and will are respected kept under control. With this in place brainwash, become the norm a new way of living and existence surrender any will pro and con from any cult member associate outside world individual. Dictator are knows to have the give of speech one word become a sharp knife invisible use to stab mentaly spiritually physically any one expose to the dictator magnetic field. Every one become like glue to the dictator words considered like prophecy sacred words eventually take over their soul like if the dictator words were the words of God itself. Words pronounced by a dictator become sword were injustice turn out in mass justice also where non-sense become the rule of life. Just like drinking cool aid eventually, the sheep less foe followers have lost their identity and faculty to think make choice render decision. For now on without any effort the leader like all dictators have upper hand to mandate how to dress to speak to eat to sleep the list goes on destroying entire life. The more power it given to one individual the more irreparable disaster catastrophic situation arises among the cult under the rule of a dictator resulting chaos disorder left unfinished for the entire society to pick up the mess.

# Child labors

With no respect for laws family and the society cult form rule that are very strict have mentality close to any that do not adhere or make part of the group. Energy has to be convening toward one gold set by the leader. Dictator does not have conscience often neglect their own responsibility to project them upon faithful suborned delegate. Feed from free labors of adult also children's the leader acknowledge nothing careless about the age of his "thing" and have no feeling toward nothing in the outside but himself. Long hour in the heat during summer during winter time hour spend on the cold make no difference as for the leader feel in control and the only one given orders. When cult starts are for the most part very small and poor this creates different stage of abuse neglect cruelties. Consider like slave at young age children's are force to work in the field picking up rock regardless if boys or girls are sick in pain not feeling good. No question no time for sport evil invention and loss of time the only thing that count is what benefit to the leader. It's a yes to all order like army wise there is no do not want gladder yes sir to everything. Children's are condition ate to believe that their suffering and labor is the greatest thing they could ever do on earth that their sacrifices sorrow labor well worthy. When is time to give them some artificial "luxury" the leader make sure to take advantage of the situation in one hand he give with the other he retrieve. Interest drove private organization especially when the same organization builds up wall where all controlled as much as individual then literature mail friend contact with the exterior. Labor is a key number one for any dictator to gain control and upper hand upon his folks. The more the faithful are busy connect the less time they have to stop think to the present situation. By keeping everybody busy and ensure that no time allowed that would open door to recollection take conscience crisis the dictator leader as free hand card in his hand. He is the winner in all situations because the leader came to find out that when people are busy and tired they usually do not take time to think rather surrender. Nothing easier for anyone to conquer "thing" what really are kids to cemented foundation with false ideology using intimidation force rarely kindness to improvise free way for victory. There is not one-day pass by without exhortation toward a more generous giving. For the leader dictator noting surpass his temporary authority. Situation becomes occasion that lead to opportunities. Kids in this ambiance already hurt physically emotionally beyond words spoken incommensurable suffering trauma the one who's caring load of dishonesty in despair soon realize there not a chance for him for a bright better future. Mad man theories rule of iron-exaggerated expectation replace the common sense daddy mommy become like a figure. Family nothing but a wreck under the pressure of barrage of brainwash demand children's of cult have no chance in life. As time goes by and gets older nothing, nothing makes sense harvest hatred drive by disappointment. Use to be alone children's of cult lose all respect for their so called parent still love them in some case but nothing there to connect. Looking back at the forced hour of work abuse and negligence, the only thing comes across their mind in many time and circumstance why me? Question like dad mom what did I ever did for you to give me away. Why did I have to go through this kind of "education"? Why did you put your faith your future into the hand of a dictator? What drove your motive to give up in life? Was I so much a bother at birth so you could not handle me? Millions of time I was crying hurting begging have you ever earing me. Day in day out I was a target bullied by perpetrator among other's children's. We all had to endure the evilness this unwanted suffering labors molestation the list goes on. Where do you place yourself in this picture your honor your vows exchange the day of your wedding? Is this was the purpose of your union? Is this situation was the only perfect way to answer your call? What had stopped you to find other solution? Ignorance stupidity rejection of your obligation excuse that had giving you good conscience. For us children's of cult answer are hard to dealing with both your coward decision this include its consequence.

Will you have been happy experiencing the same treatment? Takes part in the same hour in field picking up rock pilling wood and shorting rotten vegetable? The same food was picking up from garbage to feed us on a daily basis. I am asking these few questions myself for a long time. I am sure other ex-cult children's ask themselves identical question receiving very few answer if none at all. This including the children that grows up with me in this cult colleague of misfortune. Today we still are affected by these abuses exploitation lack of education and we got older. All this forced labors these sufferings long hour of despair is the fruit the heart of the problem and why? Where you to be selfish parent you are also advance is age well comfortable in you hidden secure fortresses. This is mind control has turned you into child labors isolation abuse given to your children is your future to the society. I must conclude you must be proud of your accomplishment or just too afraid to come out of your secure zone and face reality of life. Religion is a tool used to archive and accomplish good on Earth also that have contribute to so much of misery disorder always had been overlook because it is of the domain of Faith. Most of cult ideologies is to take something good and turned into undesirable situation with lasting consequences. Once the leader have convince himself first then his sheep less followers of remedies that he's the only one to possess miraculously have the cure well the boat is aboard and floating. All matter is the sheep less to be "faithful" to his rule regulation wanted and demand. Work key the most utilize because all great fortune come from labor. Forced labor becomes a due short of respect dignity and loyalties from active members to its leader. This notion of free time never exist members have to be submit to a regime of control dictation. Children's are in the view of the leader his precious continuation and value to is organization. This is why the smaller the child is the bigger of a so call victory if for the leader. The disproportioned scale in between the leader and children's is so obvious from the exterior unfortunate not the same for the controlled interior members active of a cult. Child in a cult has to be at the potential of an adult. No time for him to develop discover possibility have a career choose friends is forbid seeded like a way of eternal damnation. This is why it is so important to realize the problematic situation before it comes too late. Exploiters will be always there to find a way to become rich powerful on the behalf of innocent person. Society need to tackle this epidemic cancer when considering its long-term effects to the victim and the common good of all citizens. If you do not experience the trauma of child abuse, you cannot comprehend the real suffering impose by force to children's of cult. This said I do not say that all organisms are the same I am speaking specific for the one that are close to the society and do not consider themselves part of it.

# *Consequences of abuses*

Speaking of the consequences of abuse, I want to say that it is the most difficult thing that victims and survivors have to confront each days of their life. The greatest challenges today as adult are to make the difference between then and now . . . It might sound funny at first reading but it is an everyday struggle to accept the abuses that took place in early childhood the devastating consequences following those abuses. Yes, the perpetrators committed crimes in our early childhood the worst has come now that we survivors are reaching the age of adulthood. See, now adult we can look back and question why? . . . When we visualize the mind of perpetrators, we attempt to understand what motivated them to perpetuate their "fantasies", all we come to see is lies and deceptions.

What turned out to be multiple series of crimes shows the survivors that they had power control over innocent's children's. Well, this happened because when we were infants a teenager the perpetrator was well in the 20's 30 at the time the abuse took place. During that period, we were not capable of defending ourselves ensure the protection of our integrity. We were very dependent upon "safe adult supervision" to protect our childhoods, which obviously was stolen from us by our abusers. "He is only a child, he won't remember!" These are words that some may recall from the mouths of theirs abusers. Their evil mindset had not considered the notion of time and its consequences, just like rejecting their own self and their responsibility.

Now role reverse. We once children's we reached the adulthood age and the perpetrators approaching their 60's 70's. The crime to consider is the long-term consequences of hate, hurt, abandonment and betrayal. The list of abuses goes on and at the time of our abuses took place our perpetrator thought and expression was indifferent stating, "He is only a child, he won't remember." My memory recall and I am sure, others does also remember these word from the mouths' of all of our abusers. Perpetrators have the same line of language and openly saying "I don't remember that, it's just not true, you invented that to get attention, poor baby, go on with your life".

In their crooked mind and following the footsteps of abusers, most perpetrator justify themselves with clean consciences. In most of case were abuses occurs the perpetrators himself had been victimize also chooses to live in denial refuse to take step remedy counseling to face their own issues. In this case, the once victim who become the perpetrator look for his victims and most of the time he chooses the same age or about the same age where his own abuse took place. That said it does not say that all victims become abusers this would be a false ideology conclusion just not fair for all victims and survivors that choose to come forward to put a stop and break the circle of abuses. It takes a lot of strength courage for a victim to come publicly and talk about their abuses. Their heroic effort to come forward and step up must be acknowledge because without their wiliness and determination the general public are not inform educated on the social effect that these abuses imposes unto individuals very much a live and part of the society.

Perpetrator wants society to accept them as normal people, and not as the monster that they surely are. They feel shot down inside and nothing can take them out because they are in a state of denial.

The need of survivors and what force them to seek for justice are driven away from them because the history of those short of abuses still are very prevalent today and at this time and place we survivors know that another child somewhere is being molested. How many more innocent children's and lives will it take before any kind of abuses and harassment will be wiped of the map? May be it is asking too much, but one thing is sure, we need to do something to prevent these kind of abuses in order to have a healthier society. Well we need to get educated on the subject and learn from the testimony suffering of all survivors and victims who chose to come forward from the point of view of a perpetrators mind. Learn from a crooked mind of perpetrator that imposes such of pain for the survivors to live with and the hurt and anguish that become a daily bread of sadness. What the survivors and victims' do not realize most of the time is that they are still in control of their life. It is up to them to take upon the challenge and step in order to change this kind of abuses and conflicts where the perpetrators become free monsters and the victim's expendables. Where the blame that belongs to the perpetrator is transfer upon the victim and affects their daily life. As always, the shame and guilt of being a victim also a survivor affect their daily relationship toward the outside world. The survivors too often are timid and fearful as for the victims on the road of recovery they are too busy in their own little world. The hurt becomes sensitive deeply embedded in time.

Isolation is the immediate "cures" that victims and survivors use to protect and comfort themselves. After all, asking oneself, "who can I trust, and when how?" Trust from birth has a major role in life it is a daily necessity. Trust in a normal development from childhood to adulthood, ordinarily results in good behavior. Lack of trust on the other hand, confused sense of it, results in troubled personality development. Perpetrators are empowered to use their influence upon the unwary all this because of their evil behavior twisted fantasies master to create chaos after chaos in the lives of their victims and survivors. Once this major key in life trust misrepresented, where are the nobleness, dignity and care of trust that is supposed to be render to each of us? . . . Take the trust away from infants and children's you will create dictators greater than Hitler these same children's will be capable of doing as much of horror as all the famous dictators that Earth had caring during the period of its existence.

As I said earlier just not because someone has been abused, does not necessarily mean they will someday become abusers. We are all born with a free will to choose to do good or evil unfortunately, the choice influenced by the deception of a victims to perpetrate another abuse occur and this is lamentable.

Where there is trust, there is peace and harmony where there is no trust there is a reign of chaos and disorder. Adults who were victims as children's where trust was shattered trough the medium of physical and sexual abuses resemble to those soldiers returning from been prisoner of war had participated in prison tortures. Terrorism breeds another form of terrorism speaking of wars here a good comparison. Veterans of wars who have been hurt may have lost an arm or a leg, but the worse loss is that of the mental incapacity to recover from the wounds of the soul. At time, sentiment of self-betrayal is greater and has a greater effect because the soul hurts more intensely than any physical loss. We need to confront this kind of trauma because abuses children's will one day become adults many will face a lifetime of confusion, poor self-esteem driven to their own destruction. However if these same children's succeed in their life, they will still be bearing their personal mark and all the secret consequences of those abuses in different degrees. Now it's the time together we can make a difference avoid other's kids from exploitation by perverted adults by all mean stepping into the swamp of physical and sexual aggression. It would serve as lesson by being more vigilant, learning from the experiences testimony of so many neglected victims. By studying making greater effort to discover the signal been on guard to any sign leading to a mind of a perpetrator, we might have a better chance to live a normal life in a much better world.

*Fundamental believe*

In a cult situation, one believes become the norm the life and the routine. No matter how stupid dominant the leader is to be respect. All cards on the table the leader cheat rob mistreat sexually abuse kids become virtue for it devoted members who interpret the leader will authorities. There only one-way to reach perfection or sainthood is to adhere at the max the will of the leader who became the only will of God on Earth. Using invention-creating prophecy citing bible quote preaching perfection is the preoccupation of all dictator and cult leader. Making promise to never been led astray when follow commend without asking question never put the leader will in doubt voluntary comply blindly with confidence. The whole preaching exhortation twisted mind control ascension is to promote the infallibility of the leader create environment where he is never found in a wrongdoing. If anything bad happened to the group especially to the leader the fault is put on the infidelity of the sheep less member's followers if something good happened well this is because of the leader cleaver and his dedication. In general cult trend to submit abide to a rule dictated by the leader to which the leader is not oblige to abide by it. He is a man of God prophet or messiah whatever title follower's décor the leader. In rare occasion, you see rarely the leader give example by promoting austerity in life prayers suffering the list goes on. Indoctrination is crucial for the growth of the cult, leader this is why children's are mistreated become a normal way of life for the parents, and adult who are member active in the compound. All effort is converge toward the success of "the work". This word is a magic phenomenon that persuades many to give their right away and freedom to tremble when the so call hand of God is about to cast then with punishment. Fear nothing more just a little finger in the air and mass of sheep less people tremble to the point the loose their sanity. Indoctrination in value believe faith moral are condition ate by a motif and this is the core of the leader ruse to reach all uncertain sheep's lost in their life. Promise of happiness peace love the list have no end and last until the sheep's surrender peacefully to his new way in life. Most of the sheep's less are individual who are facing financial conjugal relationship difficulties are on the merge to a total collapse. Cult and dictators by experience also know that at a very young age when the children now adult start in life they face much challenge. Just coming out of the net ready to affront much good and bad experience here is a fertile ground for seeding doubt exploitation and "victory." With a perfect timing and precision nothing work well then a good talker who has the ability to held his "victim" glue to his or her lips. One word become a sword well sharp driving into the soul of undecided person guide with precision right to the heart of the recipient due to a lacks of stability. Prophecy menace promise of honor responsibly is the bait cast to bring potential candidates into the world of cult and dictators. Cult leader also dictator is most likely sociopath individual who has a deviation mental but refuse to take step and remedy. They believe that the whole society is out there to get them to destroy their reputation and to demolish the "work" as if society was fulfilling with demons. No one possess the right avenue when dealing with salvation no one have authorities when dealing with the leader and dictator if it occurs then the leader or dictator label this as persecution like stolen prestige in power. Never the less when everything is fine and no problem occur well this his taking as if God is happy that the faith of active members where blessed and approve. Everything you desire or wished is be given to you only based on salvation. Faith is the motive the impulsion in the daily practice sacrifice to take a rapid courant for extortion and exploitation. Many of the active members slowly fully adhere to all expectations and desire of the leader in rare case some resist and rebel against such treatment. Those who have the nerve to oppose to the treatment become automatically rebel enemy of "God". Solemnly classify as traitors and for the leader regain, momentum is a challenge and with precision built up barrier by lies so the remaining of faithful are kept in the ignorance. Cult always works under cover to achieve their evilness always in vigilance to overlook at their success of their master piece which is the destruction of society rupture of family under the guise of false believe and cover up.

*Sings of cults*

Very well calculated and organize these group cult and false religion are altogether follows identical rule and regulation. Even if they are separated by long distance or exist nearby they do the same "work" the same mentality and practice the same believe. One may have different rule and presentation but the essence is identical to all others cults. First to be an inclusive part of a cultic organization you have to trend toward "perfection". In a cult you do not have the right to think nor ask any question. Everything is govern and dictated on a daily basis so every movement tendency and result does not interfere with the "will of God" that is solely represented by the orders given by the leader. Blind obedience and submission is a must or you get ready to face the consequences. Only the leader is guided and illuminated directly by God there are no place for a "no" everything is a "yes" event if what is asked is representable by laws or by conscience. Perfection is key number one in the demand of the leader because the leader knows that if he succeeds to brainwash his followers with this unachievable gold then he win and have every one of his sheep less followers in the palm of his hand. This is the must do and there is no other way possible and livable if you want to be call noble faithful and elites. Menaces also rarely at time use are glories initiated as a will of God and manner of salvation and eternal guaranties of beatitudes. To who ever want to separate he or herself from the movement this become a source of damnation humiliation also rejection. Once you cross the door and recover from their rule and will the more you become an outsider and the more the remaining of the sheep less are warned to be on the lookout and prohibit to address any word or conversation with the bad example ex-members. In this atmosphere and style the leader keep a perfect control over every little movement and say of his supporters. This brings parents members active living under the roof of the cult to denied the basic right to their own blood and flesh. Cults are a mental conditioning freak of governing and ruling over the leader figuring views bunch of globule honest desperate in most of the time in financial familial status and faith troubled human being and master to render them like robots ready to obey on commend. There is no such of family life nor spirit by fear of indiscretions that potentially could bring harsh and be brought to justice. Blind obedience is a prime and must to be incorporated into these short of organizations. Under false believe and promises of happiness success guide under a daily schedule and vigilantly guard by zealots the leader reassure himself that his victims are a no return and hostage to his will and desire. This is a structure of evilness and realization of oneself proclaims savior lord and master. Notice that everything is under cover of the will of God despite natural laws and regulation everything is to render glory and victory to the leader considered as god himself. Faith becomes bait and a must in daily occupations routine expectations demand and orders. This is where leaders of cult are so strongly exigent toward their faithful members in the creation of their own dreams and caprices. Only leader are guide and smart enough to dictate on how a daily living family style is to be adopted. This brings to the total dislocation of entire family and assures that no matter how bad situation may become "discretion" would be a prime secure and affective resources in case where someone decide to leaks out information's. So now in this environment create a pat to invisible mental doors that progressively are far more easily to be adding on and protected. As for the parent to even want to take on their responsibility it become in their eyes impossible and in their view does make any sense bring them to reject their only duty as responsible parent to adopt a do not desire and wanted anymore. Only the leader as the knowledge the miraculous touch and precision that could give their children's the right to live exist also receive education. It's like to be hypnoses and taking over with lawful and successful art of constant work mind drilling to become into what eventually in the view of these parents the norm and definition of good and bad behaviors. The leader become the Law and the ultimate gold for sacrificing their child's their times their carrier their love and the solid education of their natural born children's. In the jungle more less present these parent loose contacts with feeling also reality eventually are predispose to the ultimate sacrifice if the will of God demanded. If you refuse to be a good example, then you will serve as a horrible warning. The gospel the bible the scripture are the tool exploited to build efficiently mental fence where pasture are clearly design like the only good food in the region and all the others nourishment poison and if desire or taken even could produce death all this because of infidelities. After this all could be said is beware of wolf disguise under the guise of sheep but in the inside are nothing more than a wolf ready to devour his victim prey.

# To Be a Parent

To be a good parent is a joyful responsibility
To be a good parent is to be present reliable
To be a good parent is create own longevity
To be a good parent is provide living viable.

To be call mother is be every minute present
To be call mother is be to children attentive
To be call mother is a timely educator spent
To be call mother is a warm home incentive.

To be call father is play the role of protector
To be call father is lead ways to respect love
To be call father is a strong family connector
To be call father is to teach what is truelove.

Nobles of family is future Universe growth
Nobles of family is to take charge to educate
Nobles of family is fidelity in solemn troth
Nobles of family are as children's emulate.

*Confidence*

Walk confidently toward
The direction of your dreams
Reach for the star your rewards
Live joyful the life you esteem
You imagine having to pursue
Enjoy life that you do imagine
Simplify it course is a must do
Independently be imaginative
Creative spontaneous courageous
Tackle all adversity with force

Don't saddle out be advantageous
The entire Laws of the Universe
Would be simpler not outrageous
Paradise will soon be in it full bloom
Dispensing rainbow of peace and joy
Place Serenity harmonies radiation zooms.
For eternity embrace grace fullness to enjoy